Contents

Table of Contents

Practice Book

Grade 1

Harcourt

Orlando   Austin   Chicago   New York   Toronto   London   San Diego

Visit *The Learning Site!*
www.harcourtschool.com

Name _____

▶ **Draw a line to match each word to a picture.**

class

teacher

school

To the Teacher
Read each word aloud. Tell children to find the picture
that goes with the word. Have them draw a line from
the word to the picture.

Lesson 1: Vocabulary

Name _____

▶ **Circle the correct word. Then write it on the line.**

is   I

_____
- - - - - - - -

1. Hello, _____ am Sam.

---

class   **Miss Bell**

_____
- -

2. I am _____.

▶ **Write your name and draw a picture of yourself.**

_____
- -

3. I am _____.

Lesson 1: Language Structure
Make Introductions

To the Teacher
For items 1 and 2, read the words and sentences and guide children to complete each sentence. For item 3, have children draw themselves and complete the sentence by writing their name.

© Harcourt

Name _____

▶ **Circle the word that best completes each sentence. Write the word.**

laugh   families
_____
- -

1. Here are two _____.

my   help
_____
- - - - - - - - - - - - - - - - -

2. The girls _____ Dad.

eat   here
_____
- - - - - - - - - - - -

3. I _____ an apple.

class   talk
_____
- - - - - - - - - - - - - - - - -

4. My friend and I like to _____.

laugh   here
_____
- - - - - - - - - - - - - - - - -

5. My dog makes me _____.

To the Teacher
Read the sentences to children. Help them select the word that completes each.

Lesson 2: Vocabulary

▶ **Follow the directions as your teacher reads them.**

© Harcourt

Lesson 2: Vocabulary

8

To the Teacher
Read the directions below, and help children follow them.
Have children talk about the scene with a partner. Then
have children draw more things in the open space that
relate to Vocabulary words. 1. Circle two **families**.
2. Point to the stage. Draw something on it that will
make people **laugh**. 3. Circle two women who are
talking. 4. Draw something on the table for people to
eat. 5. Underline someone who needs **help**.

Name _____

▶ **Cut out the cards. Make sentences with the words. Match the pictures to the sentences.**

1.

My

Juan   six

is   name

2.

To the Teacher
Have children cut out the cards. On the first blank card write each child's name for them. On the second blank card have children draw their face. On the third blank card on page 10, have children write their age. Help children arrange the cards to form sentences and match the corresponding picture to each sentence. Then have them read their sentences to a partner.

Lesson 2: Language Structure
Give Personal Information

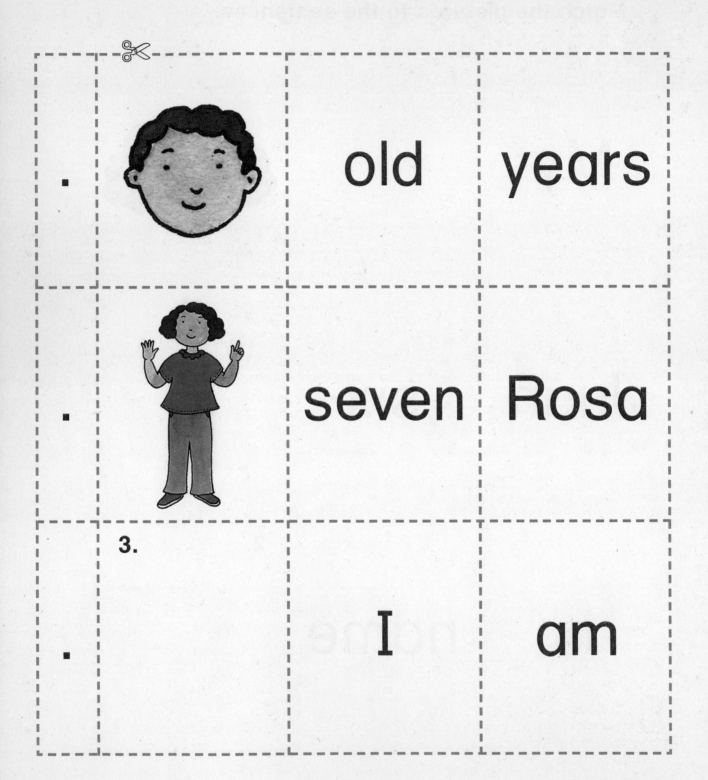

.		old	years
.		seven	Rosa
.	3.	I	am

© Harcourt

Name _____

▶ **Cut out the cards. Take turns with a partner picking a card. Do what the card says.**

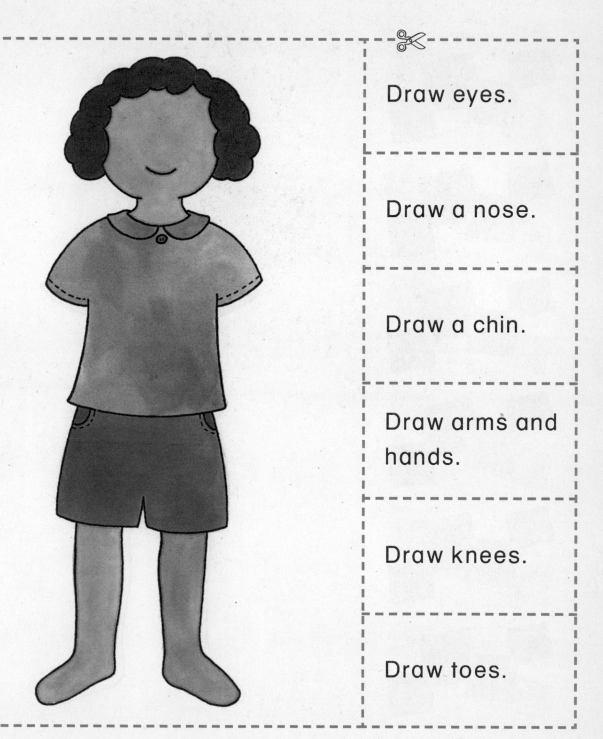

Draw eyes.

Draw a nose.

Draw a chin.

Draw arms and hands.

Draw knees.

Draw toes.

© Harcourt

To the Teacher
Have partners take turns picking a card and listen as you read it. Then have them take turns doing what it says, and returning the card to the pile. If the task on the card has already been completed, the child returns the card to the pile and misses a turn. Players can turn the page over and play again.

Lesson 3: Vocabulary

Name _____

▶ **Think about what each person says. Write a greeting or farewell in each empty speech balloon.**

Hi.   Good-bye.   Bye.   Hello.

To the Teacher
Talk about what each scene shows. Then guide children to write a greeting or farewell in each speech balloon. Pairs of children can take turns acting out the scene as a dialogue.

Lesson 3: Language Structure
Give Greetings and Farewells

Name _____

▶ **Write the word that best completes each sentence.**

| nap | swim | ride | farm |

1.

_____

- - - - - - - - - - - - - - -

I am on a _____.

2.

_____

- - - - - - - - - - - - - - -

I can _____.

3.

_____

- - - - - - - - - - - - - - -

I can _____.

4.

_____

- - - - - - - - - - - - - - -

I can _____.

Lesson 4: Vocabulary

14

To the Teacher
Read the sentences. Help children circle and write the word that completes each sentence.

Name _____

▶ **Cut out the cards. Make sentences with the words. Match the pictures to the sentences.**

✂

You	swim		.
ride	You		.
eat	You		.

© Harcourt

To the Teacher
Have children cut out the cards. Have them draw themselves swimming, riding, and eating on the blank cards. Help them use the words on either side to make sentences. Have children match the corresponding picture to each sentence. Then have the children read their sentences to a partner.

15

		swim	I
.		I	ride
.		I	eat

© Harcourt

Name _____

▶ **Cut out the cards. Match the words to the sentences. Then turn the cards over. Match them again.**

✂

team.	win!	listen.	lose.	fun!

We are a

We have to

We do not like to

We like to

We have

To the Teacher
Read the words and sentence starters with children. Then
have them cut out all the cards. Help children match the
cards to complete the sentences. Next, have them turn
the cards to the yellow side and match them again. Have
children illustrate each sentence.

Lesson 6: Vocabulary

fun!	lose.	listen.	win!	team.

	Look at my
	Hitting the ball is
	I am happy when we
	I like my friends to
	It is not fun to

Name _____

▶ **Read each sentence. Color the correct picture to match the sentence.**

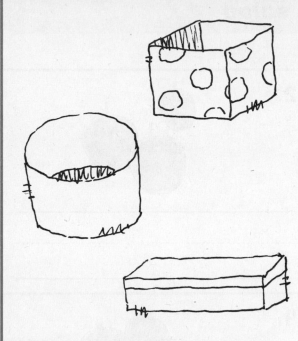

The round box is red.

The big fish is yellow.

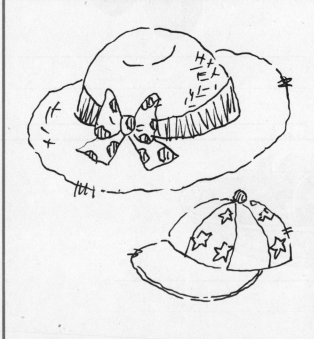

The small hat is blue.

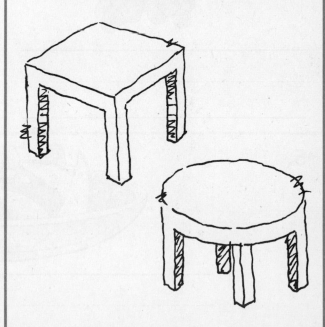

The square table is green.

To the Teacher
Read each sentence and have children color the correct object.

Lesson 6: Language Structure
Give Descriptions

Name _____

▶ **Write the picture name under the picture.**

> bananas   grapes   apples
> plums   fruit salad

1.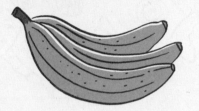

_____
- -
_____

2.

_____
- -
_____

3.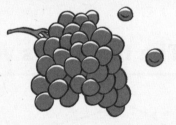

_____
- -
_____

4.

_____
- -
_____

5.

_____
- -
_____

To the Teacher
Read the words in the box and name the pictures with children. Then guide children to write the words under the matching pictures. On page 21, discuss the pictures with children. Help them to complete each sentence.

Lesson 7: Vocabulary

Name _____

▶ **Look at the pictures. Tell what is happening. Circle what you like best. Then use a word in the box to complete the sentence.**

| surprise apples grapes mix bananas |

_____

1. I like this _____ the best!

 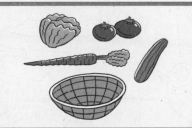 

_____

2. I would like to _____ these things.

  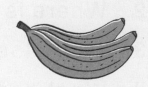

_____

3. I like to eat _____.

Lesson 7: Vocabulary

© Harcourt

Name _____

▶ **Listen as your teacher reads the directions.**
Then follow the directions.

1. Where is the bird? Color the bird yellow.

2. Where is the tree? Color the tree green.

3. What does the boy have? Color the apple red.

4. What does the girl have? Color the balloon purple.

To the Teacher
Read the questions and directions. Guide children to answer each question and follow the directions. Then invite volunteers to follow the same pattern to ask questions and give directions about other items on the page.

Lesson 7: Language Structure
Ask and Answer Questions

© Harcourt

Name _____

▶ **Cut out the pictures. Match them to a riddle.**

1. We are very small. We build anthills.	2. We fly in the sky. We build nests.
3. I can bark. I am a good pet.	4. We have wide tails. We are brown.
5. We are very big. We live near a river.	6. This is what you feel for your family.

 birds beavers ants hippos love  dog

To the Teacher
Read the riddles with children and help them to match the pictures to the riddles. On page 24 guide children to work with a partner to place the animals in the scene. Model for them how to give directions. For instance, *Put the birds in the tree; Make the birds fly to their nest.*

Lesson 8: Vocabulary

Name _____

▶ **Work with a partner. Take turns giving directions about where to put the animals.**

24

Name _____

▶ **Look at the pictures and read the words.**
Use the words to tell about the pictures.

cook	help	sweep	rake
cooks	helps	sweeps	rakes

families

teacher

friends

girl

boys

To the Teacher
Read the words in the box and have children repeat.
Then discuss the pictures and read the picture labels as
children repeat. Guide children to use present tense to
say complete sentences about each picture. Help them
use the words and labels. You may wish to have children
work with a partner.

© Harcourt

Lesson 8: Language Structure
Talk About the Present

Name _____

▶ **Look at each picture. Write a word from the box to complete the sentence.**

| wall | three | together | fall | smiled |

1. They sit _____ .

2. He does not want to _____ down.

3. Two birds are on the _____ .

4. She got _____ hats.

© Harcourt

To the Teacher
Read the words and sentences with children. Guide them to complete each sentence. Tell children that one word will not be used.

Name _____

▶ **Cut out the sentences. Match each sentence to a picture.**

bookshelf

The pencils are in the blue box.

classroom

I have a blue crayon.

crayon

The classroom has green walls.

pencils

The bookshelf has two shelves.

To the Teacher
Have children cut out the cards. Name the pictures and read the sentences with children. Guide them to match the pictures and sentences. Then have them turn the cards over. Read the sentences and have children draw and color items to match each sentence.

Lesson 9: Language Structure
Describe School Surroundings

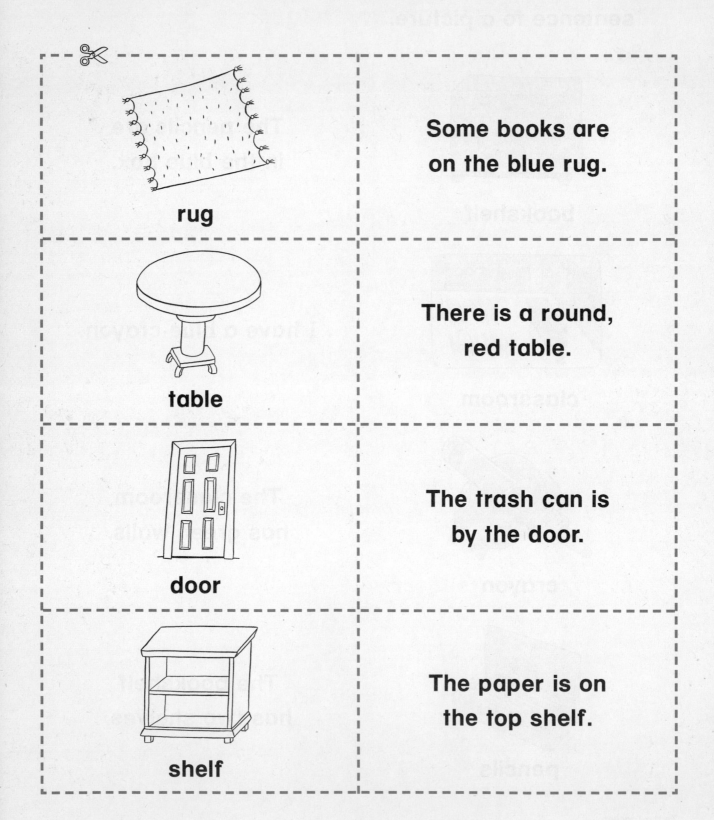

rug

Some books are
on the blue rug.

table

There is a round,
red table.

door

The trash can is
by the door.

shelf

The paper is on
the top shelf.

Name _____

 **Cut out the pictures. Paste each one next to the sentence that tells about it.**

1. I can **kick** a ball.	
2. I can **paint** a picture.	
3. I can **read books**.	
4. I can smell the **flowers**.	
5. I can play **soccer**.	

To the Teacher
Read the sentences with children. Guide children to match each picture with the corresponding sentence. Then have children turn their paper over and trace and write each Vocabulary word.

Lesson 11: Vocabulary

▶ **Trace and write each Vocabulary word.**

1. kick _____ _____

2. paint _____ _____

3. books _____ _____

4. flowers _____ _____

5. soccer _____ _____

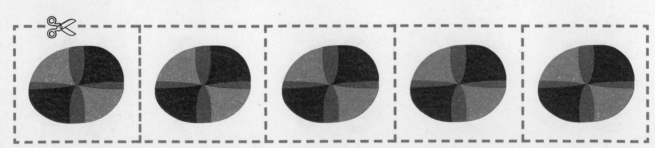

© Harcourt

Name _____

▶ **Cut out the pictures and sort them. Then tell a partner what you like and what you don't like.**

I like _____.	I don't like _____.

✂

books	pizza	apples	soccer	baseball
spiders	dolls	cars	rain	salad

To the Teacher
Have children cut the out the pictures and sort them according to their likes and dislikes. Help them to use the sentence frames as prompts to discuss their likes and dislikes with a partner. Then guide children to write corresponding sentences on the back.

Lesson 11: Language Structure
Express Likes and Dislikes

► **Write some sentences about what you like and what you don't like.**

_____

- -

_____

- -

_____

- -

_____

- -

_____

- -

_____

Name _____

▶ **Write words from the box to name the pictures.**

pet	eggs	baby chick

1. _____

2. _____

3. _____

To the Teacher
Help children read the words in the box. Discuss what
each picture shows. Have children write the word or
words to name each picture. Ask children to tell a story
to go with the pictures.

33

Lesson 12: Vocabulary

Name _____

▶ **Look at the picture. Then complete the sentences.**

| Thank you | Yes | please | You're welcome |

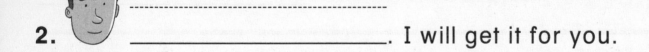

1. May I _____ see the rabbit?

2. _____. I will get it for you.

3.

4.

Lesson 12: Language Structure
Make and Answer Requests

To the Teacher
Talk about what happens in the pictures on pages 34 and 35. Help children complete the sentences to show what the people are saying. Work with them to act out each scene.

Yes   Thank you   You're welcome   please

_____

----

5. May I _____ have some plums?

_____

----

6. _____. I will get some for you.

7. _____ _____

_____ _____.

8. _____ _____

_____ _____.

Lesson 12: Language Structure
Make and Answer Requests

Name _____

▶ **Read the words. Look at the pictures. Write a word from the box to tell about each picture.**

Hello   Good-bye   Winter   Spring   Snow

_____

_____ is here.

_____

_____ is fun to play with!

_____

_____ is here.

_____

_____!

_____

_____.

To the Teacher
Discuss the pictures. Help children choose and write the correct word for each picture.

© Harcourt

Name _____

▶ **Cut out the cards. Read the words. Add <u>ed</u> and <u>ing</u> to make new words.**

jump		snow		
play		rain		
talk		plant		
mix		fish		
pick		walk		

ed	ed	ed	ed	ed
ing	ing	ing	ing	ing

To the Teacher
Help children read the action words. Then have them cut out all the cards. Show them how to use the *ed* and *ing* cards to make new words. Help them use the new words to tell about the past.

37

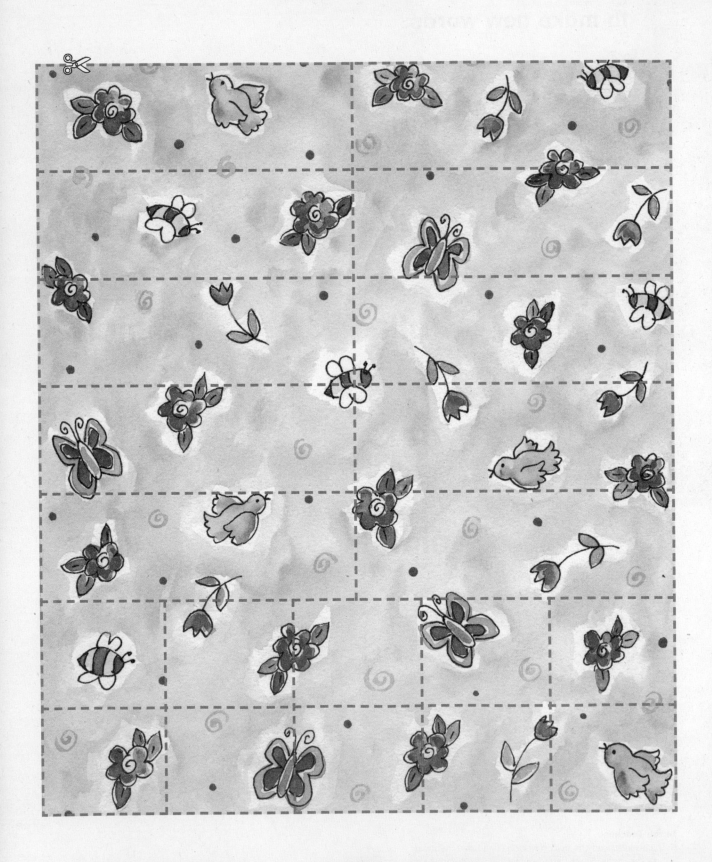

Name _____

▶ Cut out the riddles. Cut out the pictures and the words. Use the pictures and words to answer the riddles.

✂ -

1. You put us in a hole. What are we?	2. I shine in the sky. What am I?
3. I fall from the sky. What am I?	4. You walk on me. What am I?
5. I grow from a seed. What am I?	6. I am all around you. What am I?
7. We grow underground. What are we?	8. We grow on a stem. What are we?

seeds	roots 
leaves 	sun
plant 	air 
ground	rain 

To the Teacher
Have children cut out the riddles and glue them in order on art paper. Then have children cut out the pictures and words. Read the riddles. Have children glue the pictures and words beside the riddles as answers.

Lesson 14: Vocabulary

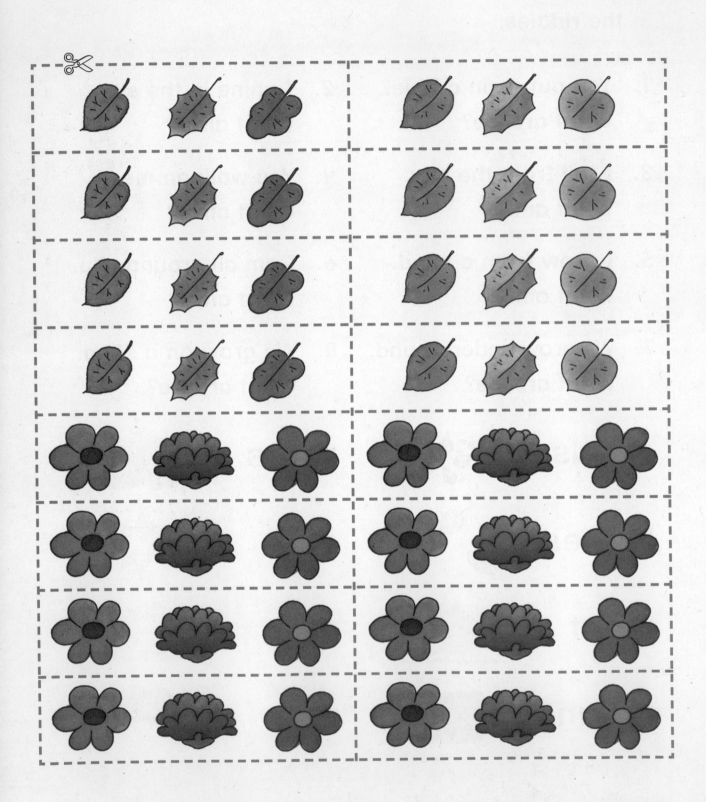

Name _____

► **Cut out the pictures. Put them in the right order.**

© Harcourt

To the Teacher
Have children cut out the pictures in each row. Have
them arrange the pictures in an order that makes sense.
Talk about the events, using the words *first*, *next*, *then*,
and *last*.

Lesson 14: Language Structure
Describe Sequence

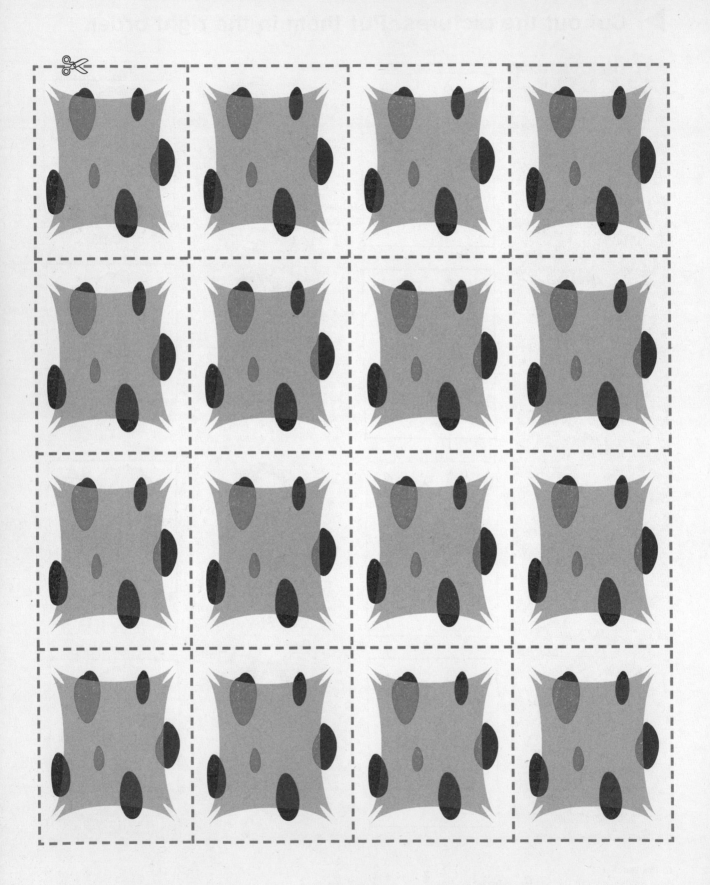

Lesson 14: Language Structure
Describe Sequence

Name _____

▶ **Complete each sentence with a word from the box. Cut out the cards. Match the sentences with the pictures.**

| high | stretch | fly | sky | pretend | try |

✂

_____

I can _____ my arms.

_____

The sun is up in the _____.

_____

I can _____ to be a cat.

_____

A bird can _____ up to a tree.

_____

I will _____ to hit the ball.

_____

The box is up too _____.

To the Teacher
Help children read each sentence, identify the missing
word, and write it on the lines. Then have children cut
out the cards and match the sentences with the pictures.

Lesson 16: Vocabulary

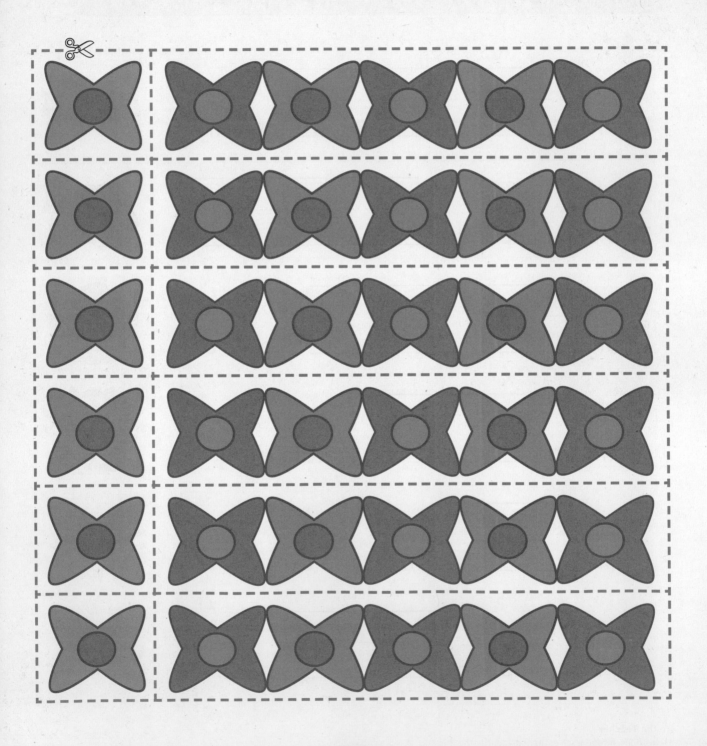

Name _____

▶ **Read the sentences and follow the directions.**

1. **Color the ball that is smaller.**

2. **Color the bird that is higher.**

3. **Color the turtle that is slower.**

4. **Color the jet that is lower.**

5. **Color the horse that is faster.**

6. **Color the shoe that is bigger.**

To the Teacher
Read the sentences. Help children identify the correct
objects they are to color.

Lesson 16: Language Structure
Make Comparisons: -er, -est

Name _____

▶ **Write a word to finish the sentences.**

middle	fixed	loud	television

1. Let's watch _____.

2. I'll sit in the _____.

3. I hear a _____ sound.

4. The TV needs to be _____.

© Harcourt

To the Teacher
Discuss the pictures on pages 46–47. Then help children
choose the word that best completes each sentence.

Okay	Tomorrow	week	Maybe

_____

- -

5. _____ we should play a game.

_____

- -

6. _____! Let's play a game.

_____

- -

7. _____ I will take the TV to be fixed.

_____

- -

8. It will be fixed next _____.

Lesson 17: Vocabulary

Name _____

▶ **Look at the picture and complete each sentence.**

many	big	little	under

1. There are _____ kittens in the box.

2. The cat is _____ the table.

3. The dog has a _____ blue hat.

4. The mouse has a _____ bell.

To the Teacher
Help children to describe the picture. Then guide them
to complete the sentences.

© Harcourt

Name _____

► **Write a word to finish each sentence.**

| artist   tools   builds   makes   pictures   use |

_____

----

1. Artists _____ tools.

_____

----

2. Brushes and pliers are _____.

_____

----

3. This artist _____ a bowl.

_____

----

4. This artist _____ things.

_____

----

5. Do you paint _____?

_____

----

6. You are an _____ too!

To the Teacher
Have children read the words in the box. Read the
sentences with children. Talk about what each picture
shows. Then have children choose a word that completes
the sentence and write it on the line.

49

Name _____

▶ **Draw something to match each phrase.**

1. as big as a house

2. as small as a mouse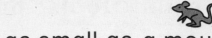

3. as hard as a rock

4. as soft as a kitten

5. as straight as a line

6. as round as a circle

To the Teacher
Read the phrases to children. Have them draw pictures
to show something that corresponds to each phrase.
Have children use the language pattern to tell about
each picture.

Name _____

▶ **Use a word from the box to complete each sentence.**

| library crops stories born job |

1. A baby is _____ .

2. Teaching is her _____ .

3. It's time to pick the _____ .

4. Grandpa is telling _____ .

5. The _____ has books.

To the Teacher
Read the sentences with children. Help them to
complete each sentence with a word from the box.

Lesson 19: Vocabulary

© Harcourt

Name _____

▶ **Write Today or Yesterday to complete each sentence.**

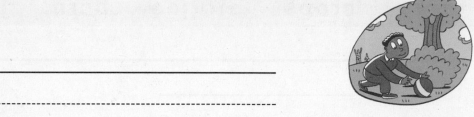

1. _____ I played with a ball.

2. _____ we look at my book.

3. _____ I played outside.

4. _____ we clap our hands.

Lesson 19: Language Structure
Talk About the Past

To the Teacher
Read the sentences with children. Help children
complete each sentence by writing *yesterday* or *today* at
the beginning.

Name _____

▶ **Cut out each place. Paste it above its name.**

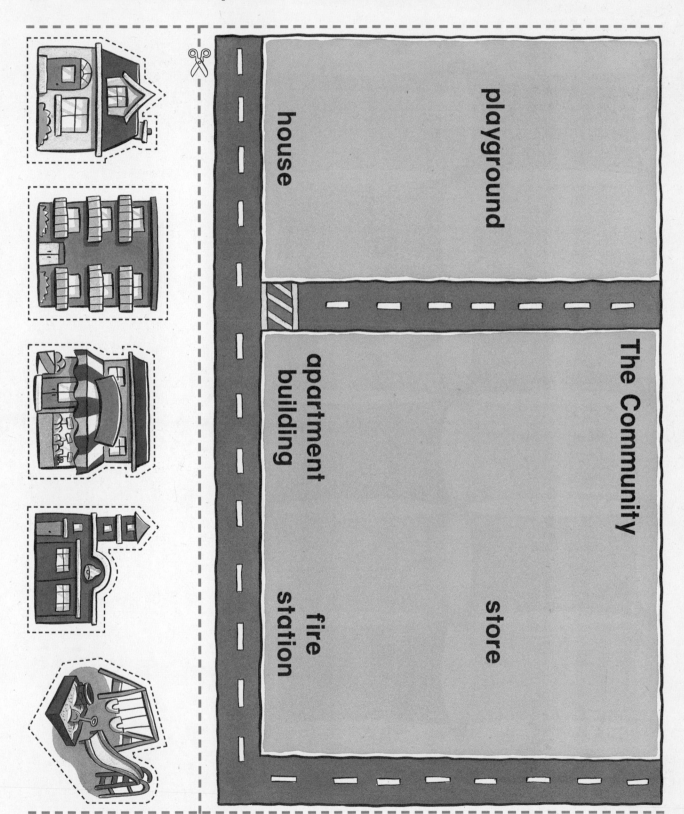

To the Teacher
Have children identify each of the community places
and cut them out. Read aloud the heading and labels
on the page. Have children paste each picture above the
appropriate label.

53

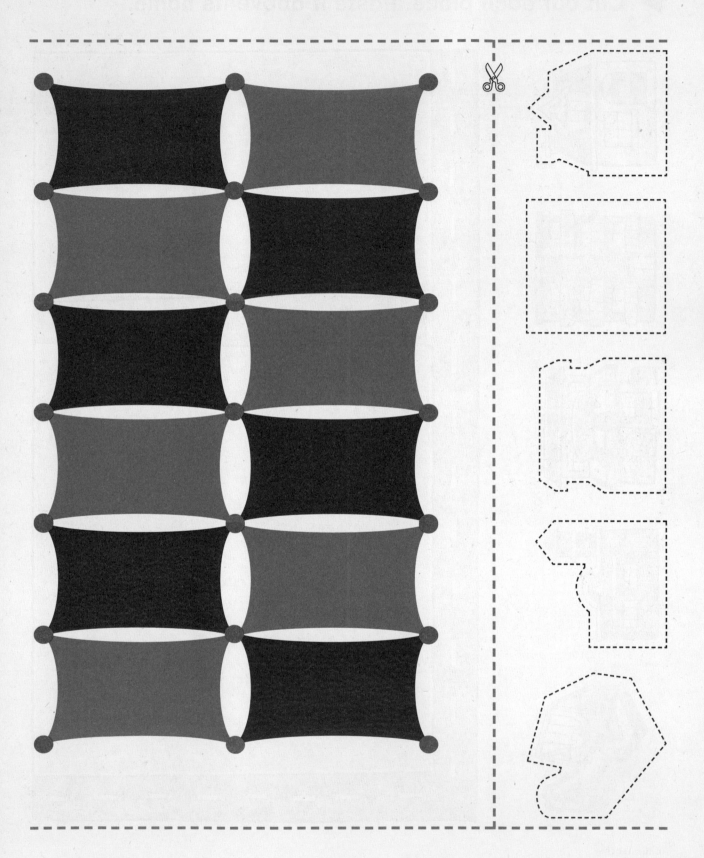

Name _____

▶ **Choose the word that best completes each sentence.**

Nate   Nate's

_____
- - - - - - - - - - - - - - - - -

1. This is _____ house.

Nate   Nate's

_____
- - - - - - - - - - - - - - - - -

2. _____ mom works here.

Her   His

_____
- - - - - - - - - - - - - - - - -

3. _____ dad works at a store.

---

her   their

_____
- - - - - - - - - - - - - - - - -

4. Sam is _____ dog.

To the Teacher
Read aloud the first item on the page and the answer
choices. Have children decide which choice is correct
and write the word on the line. Continue with other
examples on the page.

Lesson 21: Language Structure
Talk About Possession

Name _____

▶ **Draw a line to connect each question to the matching picture.**

1. Who needs a **shoe**? ●	● 
2. Who will **share** a toy? ●	● 
3. Who works in the **town**? ●	● 
4. Who needs a **bath**? ●	● 
5. Who makes **bread**? ●	●

Lesson 22: Vocabulary

To the Teacher
Read each question aloud with children. Guide them as they draw a line to the picture that answers the question.

Name _____

▶ **Cut out the cards. Use them to build sentences.**

.	I	like	need
want			

To the Teacher
Read the words with children. Identify the pictures. Have children cut apart the words and pictures to build and read sentences. Children can draw pictures in the blank sections to build new sentences.

57

Lesson 22: Language Structure
Express Needs, Desires, and Preferences

| need | like | We | a |
| | | want | |

© Harcourt

Name _____

▶ **Use a word from the box to complete each sentence.**

lion	female	dinner	cub	male

1. I am a boy.

_____

I am a _____.

2. I am a girl.

_____

I am a _____.

3. I am a wild baby lion.

_____

I am a _____.

4. I eat supper.

_____

I eat _____.

To the Teacher
Read the sentences aloud with children. Help them complete each sentence with a Vocabulary word. Then complete the Vocabulary exercise on page 60.

59

Lesson 23: Vocabulary

© Harcourt

▶ **Write a Vocabulary word in each web.**

lion   dinner   male   female

_____

Wild
Animals

beaver   hippo

_____

Meals

lunch   breakfast

brother   cousin

_____
----

friend   Dad

sister   aunt

_____
----

grandma   Mom

To the Teacher
Read the webs with children. Guide them to write a
Vocabulary word to complete each web.

Name _____

▶ **Cut out the cards. Use them to build sentences.**

get	please	.	.
point	me	the
to	go	

© Harcourt

To the Teacher
Read the words and name the pictures with children.
Help them cut out the cards and use them to build
commands.

Lesson 23: Language Structure
Give Commands

.	.	Please	Get
the	him	Look
	Go	at

© Harcourt

Name _____

▶ **Write a word to complete each sentence.**

| catch   park   wish   lost   city   swings |

1. Many people live in a _____ .

2. Flowers grow in the _____ .

3. I can _____ the ball.

4. We play on the _____ .

5. I _____ my shoe.

6. I _____ for a new bike.

To the Teacher
Read aloud the words in the box and the sentences with children. Have them look at the picture clue and complete each sentence with a Vocabulary word. Then complete the Vocabulary exercise on page 64.

Lesson 24: Vocabulary

© Harcourt

▶ **Write a word to name each picture.**

catch   city   park   swings   wish

To the Teacher
Read the words in the box with children. Talk about what is happening in the scene. Have children write a word from the box to label each picture.

© Harcourt

Name _____

▶ **Cut out the cards. Use the words to tell your partner where to put Chip.**

behind   **by**   **in**

© Harcourt

To the Teacher
Have children cut out the picture of Chip and the word cards. Have partners take turns using the words to tell each other where to put Chip, for example, *under the table, near the chair, by the door.* Children can turn over the page and continue the game with the park scene.

Lesson 24: Language Structure
Follow and Give Directions

near   on   under

Lesson 24: Language Structure
Follow and Give Directions

Name _____

▶ **Cut out the cards. Put them together to build sentences.**

✂

 The **world** | is **tall**.

 The shoe | is **young**.

 The pencil | is round.

 The baby | is **big**.

 The giraffe | is **old**.

 The elephant | is **happy**.

 The boy | is **short**.

To the Teacher
Read the phrases with children. Guide them to build
sentences. Then have children write their own phrases
on the blank sides of the cards and build more
sentences. There will be more than one correct answer.

Lesson 26: Vocabulary

✂

is **tall**.

is **young**.

is round.

is **big**.

is **old**.

is **happy**.

is **short**.

Name _____

▶ **Write the word that tells when you do each thing.**
Talk to a partner about the pictures and words.

| morning | afternoon | evening | night |

1.

_____

2.

_____

3.

_____

4.

_____

© Harcourt

To the Teacher
Discuss each picture with children. Guide them to think about the time of day they do each thing and help them write the corresponding word under each picture. Then have them say a sentence that tells about each picture.

Lesson 26: Language Structure
Describe Routines

Name _____

▶ **Write each word under the picture it tells about. Tell a partner about each picture.**

| earth | melt | push | strongest |

1.

_____
- -
_____

2.

_____
- -
_____

3.

_____
- -
_____

4.

_____
- -
_____

To the Teacher
Have children write each word under the corresponding picture. Then have children work with a partner to say a sentence about each picture.

© Harcourt

Name _____

▶ **Cut out the pictures. Put them in order. Tell a partner about the pictures.**

big	thicker	small
thick	smaller	thickest
bigger	smallest	biggest

To the Teacher
Have children cut out the cards and arrange the pictures
in order. Have them use comparing words to tell a partner
about the pictures. Then have children turn the cards
over. Read the words with children and have them draw
corresponding pictures.

71

Lesson 27: Language Structure
Make Comparisons: -er, -est

© Harcourt

tall	taller	tallest
cold	**colder**	**coldest**
long	**longer**	**longest**

Name _____

▶ **Match each sentence with a picture.**

✂

 **Astronauts**	**rocks**	**moon**
explore	**Hills**	**Mountains**
I like to _____ new places.	You can find _____ **outside**.	_____ are smaller than **mountains**.
_____ travel in space.	The _____ shines at night.	_____ are taller than **hills**.

To the Teacher
Have children cut out the cards. Read the sentences
with children and guide them to match the pictures and
sentences.

Lesson 28: Vocabulary

Name _____

▶ **Write the sentence that tells about the picture.**

1. _____

     I eat.   **I will eat.**

2. _____

    I throw the ball.   **I will throw the ball.**

3. _____

    I will sleep.   **I sleep.**

To the Teacher
Discuss each picture with children, and read the
sentences. Help children decide which sentence matches
each picture.

Lesson 28: Language Structure
Talk About the Future

Name _____

▶ **Follow the directions.**

1. Color the **sea** blue.

2. Draw some toy **boats sailing** down the **river**.

3. Circle the **island**.

4. Draw a hot dog **cooking** in the pan.

5. Make the boy's face look **scared**.

6. Draw the girl's **dreams**.

To the Teacher
Read the directions to the children and guide them to
follow each.

© Harcourt

Name _____

▶ **Cut out the cards. Use them to build sentences.**

they	we	happy	I feel	.
sad	should	sleepy	I think	.
good	she	will	have fun	!
go to school		go to my house		!
have a picnic		play a game		.

To the Teacher
Have children cut out the words and form sentences. Guide
them to read the sentences with a partner. You may wish to
have them match their sentences to the picture cards on
Teacher Resource Book page 64 or draw their own pictures to
go with their sentences.

Lesson 29: Language Structure
Express Ideas and Feelings

.	dance	go	hungry	scared
.	watch	sleep	excited	play
.	read	are	silly	run
!	go outside		I feel	
!	eat lunch		I think	

© Harcourt

Phonics Practice Pages

Name _____

▶ **Circle the picture if its name begins with /m/.**
Then write the letter m under the picture.

1.	2.	3.

4.	5.	6.

7.	8.	9.

10.	11.	12.

To the Teacher
Read aloud the directions and help children name each picture. Complete items 1–3 with children to be sure they understand the directions.

Name _____

▶ **Circle the picture if its name begins with the short *a* sound—/a/. Then write the letter *a* under the picture.**

1.	2.	3.
4.	5.	6.
7.	8.	9.

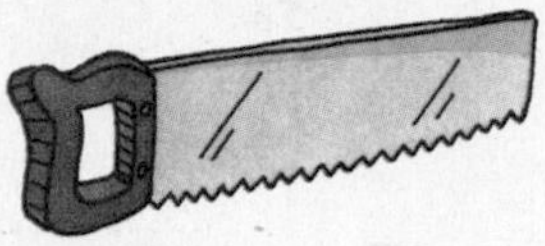

© Harcourt

To the Teacher
Read aloud the directions and help children name each
picture. Complete items 1–3 with children to be sure
they understand the directions.

Name _____

▶ For 1–6, circle the picture whose name begins with /s/. Then trace and write the letter s. For 7, draw pictures whose names begin with s.

1.
_____
S _ _ _ _ _ _ _

2.
_____
S _ _ _ _ _ _ _

3.
_____
S _ _ _ _ _ _ _

4.
_____
S _ _ _ _ _ _ _

5.
_____
S _ _ _ _ _ _ _

6.
_____
S _ _ _ _ _ _ _

7.
_____
S _ _ _ _ _ _ _

To the Teacher
Read aloud the directions and help children name each picture. Complete items 1–2 with children to be sure they understand the directions. For item 7, brainstorm possible pictures with children.

Consonant /s/s

© Harcourt

Name _____

▶ **For 1–4, circle the picture whose name begins with /t/. Then trace and write the letter _t_. For 5–8, circle the picture whose name ends with /t/. Then trace and write the letter _t_.**

1.
_____
_†_ - - - - - - - - -
_____

2.
_____
_†_ - - - - - - - - -
_____

3.
_____
_†_ - - - - - - - - -
_____

4.
_____
_†_ - - - - - - - - -
_____

5.
_____
- - - - - - - _†_ - -
_____

6.
_____
- - - - - - - _†_ - -
_____

7.
_____
- - - - - - - _†_ - -
_____

8.
_____
- - - - - - - _†_ - -
_____

To the Teacher
Read aloud the directions and help children name each
picture. Complete items 1 and 5 with children to be sure
they understand the directions.

Consonant /t/t

Name _____

▶ **Circle the picture if its name begins with /k/.**
Then write the letter _c_ under the picture.

1. 	2. 	3. 
4. 	5.	6. 
7. 	8. 	9.

To the Teacher
Read aloud the directions and help children name each
picture. Complete items 1–3 with children to be sure
they understand the directions.

Name _____

▶ **For 1–4, circle the picture whose name begins with /p/. Then trace and write the letter _p_. For 5–8, circle the picture whose name ends with /p/. Then trace and write the letter _p_.**

1. p

2. p

3. p

4. p

5. p

6. p

7. p

8. p

© Harcourt

To the Teacher
Read aloud the directions and help children name each picture. Complete items 1 and 5 with children to be sure they understand the directions.

85

Consonant /p/p

Name _____

► **Circle the picture whose name begins with /h/.**
Then trace and write the letter _h_.

1. h

2. h

3. h

4. h

5. h

6. h

7. h

8. h

To the Teacher
Read aloud the directions and help children name each
picture. Complete items 1–2 with children to be sure
they understand the directions.

© Harcourt

Name _____

▶ **For 1–4, circle the picture whose name begins with /d/. Then trace and write the letter _d_. For 5–8, circle the picture whose name ends with /d/. Then trace and write the letter _d_.**

1. d _____

2. d _____

3. d _____

4. d _____

5. d _____

6. d _____

7. d _____

8. d _____

© Harcourt

To the Teacher
Read aloud the directions and help children name each
picture. Complete items 1 and 5 with children to be sure
they understand the directions.

Consonant /d/d

Name _____

▶ For 1–4, circle the picture whose name begins with /n/. Then trace and write the letter *n*. For 5–8, circle the picture whose name ends with /n/. Then trace and write the letter *n*.

1.
_____
n _____

2.
_____
n _____

3.
_____
n _____

4.
_____
n _____

5.
_____
n _____

6.
_____
n _____

7.
_____
n _____

8.
_____
n _____

Consonant /n/n

To the Teacher
Read aloud the directions and help children name each
picture. Complete items 1 and 5 with children to be sure
they understand the directions.

© Harcourt

Name _____

▶ **Circle the picture that has the short *i* sound—/i/—in the middle. Then trace and write the letter *i*.**

1. _____ *i* _____	**2.** _____ *i* _____
3. _____ *i* _____	**4.** _____ *i* _____
5. _____ *i* _____	**6.** _____ *i* _____
7. _____ *i* _____	**8.** _____ *i* _____

To the Teacher
Read aloud the directions and help children name each picture. Complete items 1–2 with children to be sure they understand the directions.

Short Vowel /i/i

Name _____

▶ **For 1–4, circle the picture whose name begins with /k/. Then trace and write the letter _k_. For 5–8, circle the picture whose name ends with /k/. Then trace and write the letters _ck_.**

1.
k _____

2.
k _____

3.
k _____

4.
k _____

5.
ck _____

6.
ck _____

7.
ck _____

8.
ck _____

To the Teacher
Read aloud the directions and help children name each picture. Complete items 1 and 5 with children to be sure they understand the directions.

Consonant /k/k, Digraph /k/ck

© Harcourt

Name _____

▶ For 1–4, circle the picture whose name begins with /l/. Then trace and write the letter *l*. For 5–8, circle the picture whose name ends with /l/. Then trace and write the letters *ll*.

1.

2.

3.

4.

5.

6.

7.

8.

To the Teacher
Read aloud the directions and help children name each picture. Complete items 1 and 5 with children to be sure they understand the directions.

Consonant /l/l, ll

© Harcourt

Name _____

▶ **Write the word that completes the sentence.**

---

sack   sock   sick

----

1. Here is a _____.

---

dot   doll   dip

----

2. Mom got me a _____.

---

tap   tip   top

----

3. Tom is on _____.

---

pot   lot   lit

----

4. Ann has a _____ of cats.

---

hop   hat   hip

----

5. We can _____.

Short Vowel /o/o

92

To the Teacher
Read aloud the directions. Talk about the pictures and read the sentences with children. Complete item 1 with children to be sure they understand the directions.

Name _____

► **Write the word that completes the sentence.**

This   Kiss   Miss
_____

1. _____ hat is big.

That   Mat   Sat
_____

2. _____ hat is not big.

kick   lick   thick
_____

3. This hat is _____.

thin   pin   tin
_____

4. That hat is _____.

Miss   This   His
_____

5. _____ is Pat's hat.

To the Teacher
Read aloud the directions. Talk about the pictures and read the sentences with children. Complete item 1 with children to be sure they understand the directions.

Digraph /th/th

Name _____

▶ **Color the object named in the sentence.**
The crayon stands for the word *color.*
It also tells you what color to use.

1. 🖍️ the big pig.

2. 🖍️ the big dog.

3. 🖍️ the log.

4. 🖍️ the pig on the log.

5. 🖍️ the tag on the bat.

6. 🖍️ the wig.

To the Teacher
Read aloud the directions. Talk about the picture with children. Help them read and follow the directions.

© Harcourt

Name _____

▶ **Write the word from the box that completes the sentence.**

| ran | rock | rod | Rick | rip |

1. Look at that _____ _____.

2. This is a _____ _____.

3. _____ has a _____.

4. I am _____ _____.

5. Pam and Rip _____ _____.

To the Teacher
Read aloud the directions. Talk about the pictures and read the sentences with children. Complete item 1 with children to be sure they understand the directions.

Consonant /r/r

Name _____

▶ **For 1–4, circle the picture whose name begins with /f/. Then trace and write the letter *f*. For 5, read the sentence. Circle the picture that goes with the sentence. Then write the sentence on the lines.**

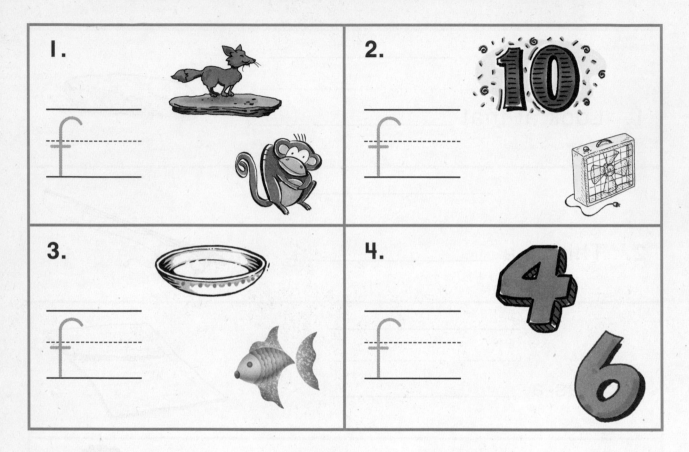

1.
f _____

2.
f _____

3.
f _____

4.
f _____

5. It is off.

_____

- -

_____

To the Teacher
Read aloud the directions. For 1–4, help children name the pictures. Complete item 1 with children to be sure they understand the directions. For 5, talk about the pictures, using the words *on* and *off*.

© Harcourt

Name _____

► **For 1–4, circle the picture whose name has the /ôr/ sound. Then trace and write the letters *or*. For 5–6, write the word that makes sense and has the /ôr/ sound.**

1.
_____
or _____

2.
_____
or _____

3.
_____
or _____

4.
_____
or _____

torn   sad   rap

_____
----
5. This is _____.

fin   for   frog

_____
----
6. This is _____ you.

To the Teacher
Read aloud the directions. For 1–4, help children name
each picture. For 5–6, talk about what is happening in
the pictures. Complete items 1 and 5 with children to be
sure they understand the directions.

R-Controlled Vowel /ôr/or

Name _____

▶ **For 1–4, circle the picture whose name begins with /sh/. Then trace and write the letters _sh_. For 5–8, circle the picture whose name ends with /sh/. Then trace and write the letters _sh_.**

1. _____ sh _____	**2.** _____ sh _____
3. _____ sh _____	**4.** _____ sh _____

5. _____ sh _____	**6.** _____ sh _____
7. _____ sh _____	**8.** _____ sh _____

To the Teacher
Read aloud the directions and help children name each picture. Complete items 1 and 5 with children to be sure they understand the directions.

© Harcourt

Name _____

1.

b

2.

b

3.

b

4.

b

5.

W

6.

W

7.

W

8.

W

To the Teacher
Read aloud the directions and help children name each
picture. Complete items 1 and 5 with children to be sure
they understand the directions.

Consonants /b/b, /w/w

© Harcourt

Name _____

▶ For 1–4, circle the picture whose name has the short e sound—/e/—in the middle. Then trace and write the letter e. For 5–6, write the word that makes sense and has the short e sound.

1. _____
   e

2. _____
   e

3. _____
   e

4. _____
   e

fan   fit   fed
_____

5. This dog likes to be _____.

walk   win   wet
_____

6. This dog is _____.

To the Teacher
Read aloud the directions. For 1–4, help children name each picture. For 5–6, talk about what is happening in the pictures. Complete items 1 and 5 with children to be sure they understand the directions.

Name _____

▶ For 1–4, circle the picture whose name begins with /ch/. Then trace and write the letters *ch*. For 5–6, write the word that makes sense and ends with /ch/.

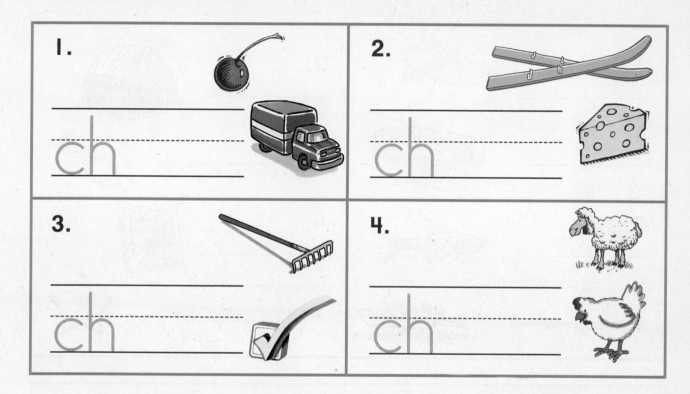

1. ‎ch

2. ‎ch

3. ‎ch

4. ‎ch

pit   pick   pitch

5. I _____ the ball.

cash   cat   catch

6. I _____ the ball.

To the Teacher
Read aloud the directions. For 1–4, help children name each picture. For 5–6, talk about what is happening in the pictures. Complete items 1 and 5 with children to be sure they understand the directions.

Digraphs /ch/*ch*, tch

Name _____

▶ For 1–4, circle the picture whose name has the /är/ sound. Then trace and write the letters *ar*. For 5–6, write the word that makes sense and begins with /y/.

1. _____ ar _____	2. _____ ar _____
3. _____ ar _____	4. _____ ar _____

born   dig   yard

5. We play in the _____.

yes   yarn   march

6. Mom made me a hat with _____.

R-Controlled Vowel /är/ar; Consonant /y/y

To the Teacher
Read aloud the directions. For 1–4, help children name each picture. For 5–6, talk about what is happening in the pictures. Complete items 1 and 5 with children to be sure they understand the directions.

Name _____

▶ **Write the word that completes the sentence.**

sit   stuck   sun
_____

- - - - - - - - - - - - - - - -

1. The _____ is out.

rug   rag   tin
_____

- - - - - - - - - - - - - - - -

2. I like this _____.

bag   bug   big
_____

- - - - - - - - - - - - - - - -

3. This _____ is small.

cat   can   cut
_____

- - - - - - - - - - - - - - - -

4. What will you _____?

fun   fat   fin
_____

- - - - - - - - - - - - - - - -

5. This is _____.

To the Teacher
Read aloud the directions. Talk about the pictures and
read the sentences with children. Complete item 1 with
children to be sure they understand the directions.

Short Vowel /u/u

Name _____

▶ **Write the word that completes the sentence.**

zip   zag   vet
_____

1. You can _____ this up.

---

just   jump   jet
_____

2. This _____ can go!

---

jog   fizz   buzz
_____

3. I can _____.

---

van   vat   jazz
_____

4. We go in the _____.

---

vest   jam   jar
_____

5. What is in the _____?

Consonants /z/z, zz; /j/j; /v/v

To the Teacher
Read aloud the directions. Talk about the pictures and read the sentences with children. Complete item 1 with children to be sure they understand the directions.

Name _____

▶ **Write the word from the box that completes the sentence.**

| fur | her | dirt | bird | burn |

1. Here is a _____.

2. The bird is in _____ nest.

3. Cats have _____.

4. Do you dig in the _____?

5. This will _____ you!

To the Teacher
Read aloud the directions. Talk about the pictures and read the sentences with children. Help them complete the sentences orally. Complete item 1 with children to be sure they understand the directions.

R-Controlled Vowel /ûr/er, ir, ur

Name _____

▶ For 1–4, circle the picture that ends with /ks/. Then write and trace the letter *x*. For 5–6, write the word that makes sense and begins with /kw/.

1. _____ ____X	**2.** _____ ____X
3. _____ ____X	**4.** _____ ____X

bark   quack   quit
_____

5. I swim and _____.

felt   quick   quilt
_____

6. Who made this _____?

To the Teacher
Read aloud the directions. For 1–4, help children name each picture. For 5–6, talk about the picture. Complete items 1 and 5 with children to be sure they understand the directions.

Name _____

▶ **Write the word that completes the sentence.**

bat   **boat**   box

1. It's fun to go in a _____.

snap   show   snow

2. Let's play in the _____.

goat   got   coat

3. This is a _____.

grow   red   road

4. The plants will _____.

slot   slow   so

5. This animal is _____.

© Harcourt

To the Teacher
Read aloud the directions. Talk about the pictures and read the sentences with children. Complete item 1 with children to be sure they understand the directions.

Long Vowel /ō/ow, oa

Name _____

▶ **Circle the picture whose name has the long *e* sound—/ē/. Then write a word from the box to name the picture.**

beet	peach	bean	tree	bee

1. _____

2. _____

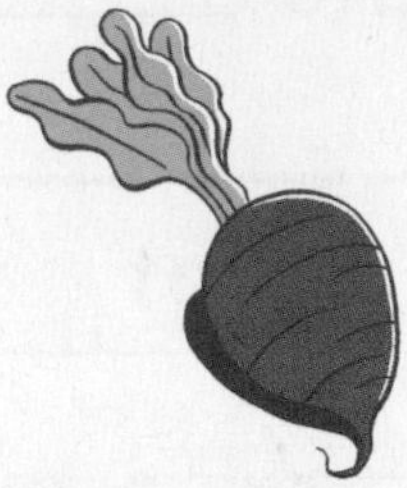

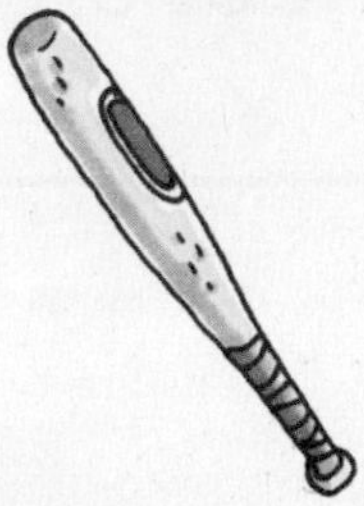

3. _____

4. _____

5. _____

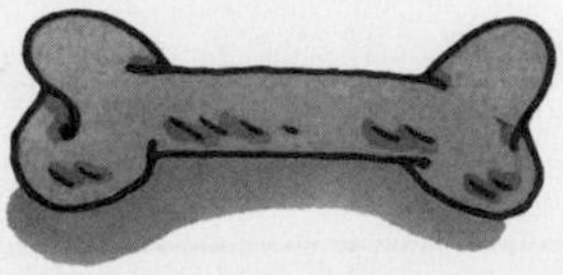

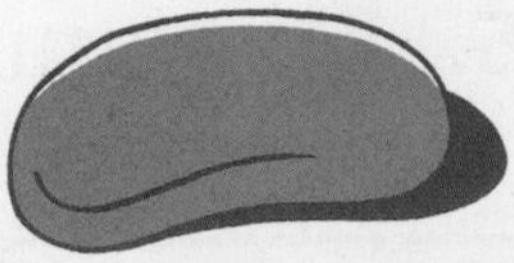

To the Teacher
Read aloud the directions and help children name each picture. Complete item 1 with children to be sure they understand the directions.

© Harcourt

Name _____

▶ **Circle the picture whose name has the long _a_ sound—/ā/. Then write a word from the box to name the picture.**

tape   lake   cane   face   plate   rake

1.

_____

- - - - - - - - - - - -

_____

2.

_____

- - - - - - - - - - - -

_____

3.

_____

- - - - - - - - - - - -

_____

4.

_____

- - - - - - - - - - - -

_____

5.

_____

- - - - - - - - - - - -

_____

6.

_____

- - - - - - - - - - - -

_____

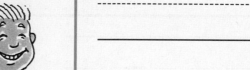

To the Teacher
Read aloud the directions and help children name each picture. Complete item 1 with children to be sure they understand the directions.

Long Vowel /ā/a-e

Name _____

▶ For 1–3, find a word in the box that tells about the picture. Write the word. For 4–6, write the word from the box that completes the sentence.

sunny   puppies   sleepy

1. _____

2. _____

3. _____

happy   Willie   funny

4. I do _____ tricks.

5. I make you _____.

6. My name is _____.

To the Teacher
Read aloud the directions. For 1–3, help children name each picture. For 4–6, talk about what is happening in the picture. Complete items 1 and 4 with children to be sure they understand the directions.

Long Vowel /ē/y, ie

© Harcourt

Name _____

▶ **Write the word that makes sense and has the long *i* sound—/ī/.**

bike   bake   beak
_____

1. I like this _____.

lane   line   land
_____

2. Can you see the _____?

tin   tame   time
_____

3. What _____ is it?

pine   pin   pane
_____

4. This is a _____ tree.

kit   kite   Kate
_____

5. The _____ is up.

To the Teacher
Read aloud the directions and help children name each picture. Complete item 1 with children to be sure they understand the directions.

Long Vowel /ī/i-e

Name _____

▶ **Write the word that completes the sentence.**

---

brown   bow   town
_____
- - - - - - - - - - - - - - - - - -

1. The dog is _____.

---

cow   owl   down
_____
- - - - - - - - - - - - - - - - - -

2. The blocks fall _____.

---

howl   clown   now
_____
- - - - - - - - - - - - - - - - - -

3. I like this _____.

---

crowd   how   cow
_____
- - - - - - - - - - - - - - - - - -

4. The _____ has spots.

---

crown   how   cream
_____
- - - - - - - - - - - - - - - - - -

5. The queen has a _____.

Vowel Diphthong /ou/ow

To the Teacher
Read aloud the directions and help children name each picture. Complete item 1 with children to be sure they understand the directions.

Name _____

▶ **Write the word that makes sense and has the long _o_ sound—/ō/.**

---

takes   drove   drops

_____

- - - - - - - - - - - - - - -

1. We _____ home.

---

sat   rod   rode

_____

- - - - - - - - - - - - - - -

2. Sam _____ his bike.

---

bond   bone   born

_____

- - - - - - - - - - - - - - -

3. The dog has a _____.

---

nose   not   nest

_____

- - - - - - - - - - - - - - -

4. Where is your _____?

---

week   woke   wag

_____

- - - - - - - - - - - - - - -

5. I just _____ up!

To the Teacher
Read aloud the directions and help children name each picture. Complete item 1 with children to be sure they understand the directions.

Long Vowel /ō/o-e

© Harcourt

Name _____

▶ **Write a word from the box to complete the sentence.**

| sky light pie high night |

_____
\- -

1. The sun is in the _____.

_____
\- -

2. Why do birds fly _____?

_____
\- -

3. Let's turn on the _____.

_____
\- -

4. Do you like peach _____?

_____
\- -

5. Now it is _____.

Long Vowel /ī/igh, y, ie

To the Teacher
Read aloud the directions and help children name each
picture. Complete item 1 with children to be sure they
understand the directions.

© Harcourt

Name _____

▶ **Write words from the boxes to name the pictures.**

snail	tray	rain

1.

_____
- - - - - - - - - - - - - - -
_____

2.

_____
- - - - - - - - - - - - - - -
_____

3.

_____
- - - - - - - - - - - - - - -
_____

sailboat	birthday	rainbow

4.

_____
- -
_____

5.

_____
- -
_____

6.

_____
- -
_____

To the Teacher
Read aloud the directions and help children name each
picture. Complete item 1 with children to be sure they
understand the directions.

Long Vowel /ā/ai, ay

Name _____

▶ **Read the sentences. Circle the sentence that tells about the picture.**

---

1. Look at that cold car!

   Look at that wild cat!

---

2. I wear a coat when it's cold.

   I can't find my old boat.

---

3. This child is ten years old.

   This child is not very old.

---

4. Bo holds a yo-yo.

   The yo-yo is green.

---

5. Frog will go up so high!

   Frog sold all the rolls.

---

6. A hippo sat on the post.

   A hippo is a kind of animal.

Long Vowels /ī/i, /ō/o

116

To the Teacher
Read aloud the directions and help children name each picture. Complete item 1 with children to be sure they understand the directions.

© Harcourt

Name _____

My Day at School	Families
class Lesson 1	families Lesson 2
school Lesson 1	help Lesson 2
teacher Lesson 1	eat Lesson 2
	talk Lesson 2
	laugh Lesson 2

To the Teacher Have children cut out the Vocabulary word cards and use them with the activities described in the *Teacher's Edition*. You may wish to have children write selected words on the blank cards.

Lessons 1 and 2: Vocabulary Word Cards

Name _____

knees

Lesson 3

hands

Lesson 3

nose

Lesson 3

chin

Lesson 3

toes

Lesson 3

arms

Lesson 3

eyes

Lesson 3

To the Teacher Have children cut out the Vocabulary word cards and use them with the activities described in the *Teacher's Edition*. You may wish to have children write selected words on the blank cards.

119

Lesson 3: Vocabulary Word Cards

© Harcourt

Name _____

Down on the Farm	Our Team
nap Lesson 4	**team** Lesson 6
swim Lesson 4	**fun** Lesson 6
ride Lesson 4	**listen** Lesson 6
farm Lesson 4	**win** Lesson 6
	lose Lesson 6

To the Teacher Have children cut out the Vocabulary word cards and use them with the activities described in the *Teacher's Edition.* You may wish to have children write selected words on the blank cards.

   Lessons 4 and 6: Vocabulary Word Cards

Name _____

A Salad Surprise

salad

Lesson 7

mix

Lesson 7

surprise

Lesson 7

fruit

Lesson 7

bananas

Lesson 7

apples

Lesson 7

grapes

Lesson 7

plums

Lesson 7

To the Teacher Have children cut out the Vocabulary word cards and use them with the activities described in the *Teacher's Edition*. You may wish to have children write selected words on the blank cards.

Lesson 7: Vocabulary Word Cards

Name _____

ants

Lesson 8

beavers

Lesson 8

birds

Lesson 8

hippos

Lesson 8

dog

Lesson 8

love

Lesson 8

To the Teacher Have children cut out the Vocabulary word cards and use them with the activities described in the *Teacher's Edition*. You may wish to have children write selected words on the blank cards.

125

Lesson 8: Vocabulary Word Cards

© Harcourt

The Big, Big Wall

wall

Lesson 9

down

Lesson 9

fall

Lesson 9

two

Lesson 9

three

Lesson 9

together

Lesson 9

smiled

Lesson 9

To the Teacher Have children cut out the Vocabulary
word cards and use them with the activities described in
the *Teacher's Edition*. You may wish to have children write
selected words on the blank cards.

127

Lesson 9: Vocabulary Word Cards

© Harcourt

Name _____

Now I Can	Dan's Pet
kick Lesson 11	**chick** Lesson 12
soccer Lesson 11	**pet** Lesson 12
paint Lesson 11	**eggs** Lesson 12
flowers Lesson 11	**baby** Lesson 12
read Lesson 11	
books Lesson 11	

To the Teacher Have children cut out the Vocabulary word cards and use them with the activities described in the *Teacher's Edition*. You may wish to have children write selected words on the blank cards.

Lessons 11 and 12: Vocabulary Word Cards

Name _____

 good-bye

Lesson 13

hello

Lesson 13

winter

Lesson 13

spring

Lesson 13

snow

Lesson 13

© Harcourt

To the Teacher Have children cut out the Vocabulary word cards and use them with the activities described in the *Teacher's Edition*. You may wish to have children write selected words on the blank cards.

131

Name _____

seeds	rain
Lesson 14	Lesson 14
plant	air
Lesson 14	Lesson 14
roots	
Lesson 14	
leaves	
Lesson 14	
sun	
Lesson 14	
ground	
Lesson 14	

© Harcourt

To the Teacher Have children cut out the Vocabulary word cards and use them with the activities described in the *Teacher's Edition*. You may wish to have children write selected words on the blank cards.

133

Lesson 14: Vocabulary Word Cards

Name _____

stretch

Lesson 16

high

Lesson 16

fly

Lesson 16

pretend

Lesson 16

try

Lesson 16

sky

Lesson 16

To the Teacher Have children cut out the Vocabulary word cards and use them with the activities described in the *Teacher's Edition*. You may wish to have children write selected words on the blank cards.

© Harcourt

135

Lesson 16: Vocabulary Word Cards

Name _____

When the TV Broke

week

Lesson 17

okay

Lesson 17

middle

Lesson 17

loud

Lesson 17

television

Lesson 17

fixed

Lesson 17

maybe

Lesson 17

tomorrow

Lesson 17

To the Teacher Have children cut out the Vocabulary word cards and use them with the activities described in the *Teacher's Edition*. You may wish to have children write selected words on the blank cards.

Lesson 17: Vocabulary Word Cards

Name _____

Tools for Artists	Tomás Rivera
artist Lesson 18	born Lesson 19
tools Lesson 18	crops Lesson 19
makes Lesson 18	stories Lesson 19
use Lesson 18	library Lesson 19
builds Lesson 18	job Lesson 19
pictures Lesson 18	

To the Teacher Have children cut out the Vocabulary word cards and use them with the activities described in the *Teacher's Edition*. You may wish to have children write a selected word on the blank card.

Lessons 18 and 19:
Vocabulary Word Cards

Name _____

What Is a Community?	Shoe Town

store
Lesson 21

shoe
Lesson 22

playground
Lesson 21

share
Lesson 22

house
Lesson 21

town
Lesson 22

apartment building
Lesson 21

bath
Lesson 22

fire station
Lesson 21

bread
Lesson 22

community
Lesson 21

© Harcourt

To the Teacher Have children cut out the Vocabulary word cards and use them with the activities described in the *Teacher's Edition*. You may wish to have children write selected words on the blank cards.

141

Name _____

lion
Lesson 23

city
Lesson 24

female
Lesson 23

lost
Lesson 24

male
Lesson 23

catch
Lesson 24

cubs
Lesson 23

park
Lesson 24

wild
Lesson 23

wish
Lesson 24

dinner
Lesson 23

swings
Lesson 24

To the Teacher Have children cut out the Vocabulary word cards and use them with the activities described in the *Teacher's Edition*.

143

Lessons 23 and 24: Vocabulary Word Cards

© Harcourt

Name _____

world

Lesson 26

tall

Lesson 26

happy

Lesson 26

young

Lesson 26

old

Lesson 26

big

Lesson 26

short

Lesson 26

To the Teacher Have children cut out the Vocabulary word cards and use them with the activities described in the *Teacher's Edition*. You may wish to have children write selected words on the blank cards.

Lesson 26: Vocabulary Word Cards

Name _____

strongest

Lesson 27

melt

Lesson 27

push

Lesson 27

earth

Lesson 27

To the Teacher Have children cut out the Vocabulary word cards and use them with the activities described in the *Teacher's Edition*. You may wish to have children write selected words on the blank cards.

147

Lesson 27: Vocabulary Word Cards

Name _____

moon

Lesson 28

hills

Lesson 28

astronauts

Lesson 28

explore

Lesson 28

rocks

Lesson 28

outside

Lesson 28

mountains

Lesson 28

To the Teacher Have children cut out the Vocabulary word cards and use them with the activities described in the *Teacher's Edition.* You may wish to have children write selected words on the blank cards.

149

Lesson 28: Vocabulary Word Cards

Name _____

cook	sea
Lesson 29	Lesson 29
river	island
Lesson 29	Lesson 29
boats	
Lesson 29	
sail	
Lesson 29	
scared	
Lesson 29	
dreams	
Lesson 29	

To the Teacher Have children cut out the Vocabulary word cards and use them with the activities described in the *Teacher's Edition*. You may wish to have children write selected words on the blank cards.

Lesson 29: Vocabulary Word Cards